FINDING
LEVEL GROUND

FINDING
LEVEL GROUND
MY JOURNEY WITH
CEREBELLAR ATAXIA

FROM VICTIM TO VICTORIOUS

BY
DEBORAH LEVI

*A bird doesn't sing
because it has an answer,*

It sings because it has a song.

Maya Angelou

TABLE OF CONTENTS

Author's Notes

My life took a dramatic turn in the 1980's. I had entered my late thirties, and each subsequent year my sense of balance worsened—slowly and steadily. Initially, my gait uncontrollably weaved to the left. All of my quick movements ended in falls, yet I refused to believe I was disabled in any way. I thought that physical limitations happened to others—not to me! Every year it grew worse and more pronounced, and by my mid-forties, I sought medical help. I received a diagnosis of cerebellar ataxia in 1994.

When the neurologist announced the test results, I had no idea what he meant. *Cerebellum* sounded like a word found in a foreign language. I never studied brain function and was unable to locate specific regions of the brain or explain their physiological functions. Since then I've learned that ataxia refers to an impaired, neurological condition with different types. I also learned the terms *degenerative disease, atrophy*, and *progressive*. My specific type of ataxia is cerebellar atrophy, a degenerative and progressive brain impairment.

I write to share a personal journey—the unraveling of my outer life and unfolding of my inner path. As effects of this disease increased I felt terribly alone, isolated, and separated from others. Those dark feelings haunted me and crept into every aspect of my life. They slowly robbed me of self-worth. Overtime I realized that they were unnecessary, unproductive, and very painful ways to feel. This is my personal story of transformation, taking place over decades, in which I learned to accept life with cerebellar ataxia. It is my slow revelation that life does not need to be lived as a victim.

Living with ataxia has guided me to share my story, to print these words. I deliver my writings both in prose and poetry. They are only intended to be personal experience that reflect my unique journey; never meant as scientific fact. My goal is threefold: to reach out and share a private struggle, to look beyond the sufferings of loss, and to encourage transformation from negative fears into positive strengths.

I invite the reader to join me on my physical, emotional, and spiritual journey. I will explore how my body continues to serve as a great teacher. I have learned that physical challenges present opportunities to use the body's signals as sacred and treasured messages. For me, the key is paying attention. I am convinced that we are much more than our physical make-up. While the body is necessary for everyday existence; it is also a wise instructor of life's mysteries.

I find it necessary to constantly examine my choices. I have learned equally from my successes and failures, the storms as well as sunny days. I believe the greatest path is from mind to heart. The challenge is to mix knowledge with compassion, to look beyond labels for life's meanings. This is my story of choice, acceptance, and trust.

I refer those who seek medical facts to texts and scientific journals. Some of these research sites are listed at the end of this book; however, many others exist. It is crucial to stay informed about reliable and relevant findings since medical information continually changes. It is my personal wish that every type of ataxia research will one day deliver hope and promise to all who suffer. I extend my gratitude to all of the dedicated researchers who are working hard to find cures. Proceeds from this book will help fund further research.

I send my words with heartfelt sincerity. May we all shed our victim-selves and grow as victors. May we remember that we are never alone. May we accept ourselves as we are.

May we all find level ground.

D.L.

Ataxia Awareness

Gradually, without warning,
my body yielded to a forceful
stranger. Like a gentle landscape
interrupted by invasive weeds,
my heart and flesh surrendered
in confusion. After increased falls,
torn muscles, weakened bones:
humiliation set in, and was tattooed

throughout my veins.
Caged by fear of rejection, I
froze, afraid to breathe. Shivering
in denial, I looked for reasons:
turned towards science. With finding
after finding, study upon study,
I slowly untangled curves and lines
of my brain's circuitry. I frequented
MRI tunnels, EEG machines,
paralyzed, terrified, afraid to wink.

After years of inner travel
on slippery dark, silent roads,
I look for level ground; paths
cemented with promise. I no
longer hear frantic voices,
thoughts no longer limit me.
Chilly air fades—I know my body
needs assistance. I wear
a shawl of acceptance

Part I

My Body is My Greatest Teacher

Finding Level Ground

1
Pre-diagnosis

Sunset Tumble

One evening in the summer of 1986, I ventured out to a tiny patch of front lawn to play a game of ball with my family. The extreme San Fernando Valley heat had become bearable and after a relatively normal day of domestic duties, relaxation was welcome. I treasured the family intimacy and was grateful to bond with my children. My older son of six years had recently been enrolled in a local park T-ball program, and was just learning the game. I took pride in demonstrating how to hit the ball and run the bases.

The role of motherhood satisfied me in multiple ways: caretaker, provider, teacher, somebody with dedication and influence. For the first thirty-six years of my life, I defined myself as a physically capable person. I was active and loved to dance. I never thought my body would be challenged in any way and did not realize how much being healthy and mobile were gifts. I since learned that every minute, every hour, every day, everything about life is a gift. Being unaware at the time, I took it all for granted.

"Put the ball on the T-stand and when you hit it, run to first base," I explained. We used the trees and bushes as markers. "I'll show you how," I instructed with confidence. However, when I attempted to run, my body would not and could not follow brain command. My legs stopped working; I fell flat on my face. My husband and two little boys ran up to me. "Are you o.k.?" they asked with true concern. "Fine! It was a hole in the grass," I replied trying to mask both my confusion and embarrassment. I blamed my tumble on the uneven ground trying to suppress my shock and disappointment. But something deep inside me knew otherwise—deep in an inner, silent place far beyond words. I had lost control of my body, and control was something important to me. I would later learn that cerebellar brain degeneration had taken root and its effects were spreading throughout my body—and my life.

For the next several years, this question "are you alright?" became common. Every time I stumbled or lost my balance, somebody asked if I needed help, and each time I became angrier and more hostile. I believed body image was crucial to my self-image, and I felt devastated that my body might be flawed in any way. My fears intensified, and my shame grew stronger year by year. As a result my self-worth decreased.

It was dark, and the day ended. Light faded; shadows lurked in the distance. The sun set.

That evening in 1986 my body failed. It crushed every future expectation I had for myself. It marked the beginning of a passage into unknown, dark, and distant territory. A new and painfully emotional and lonely journey had begun. As I retreated into the house after my fall, a familiar voice of victim mixed with self-pity raged within, while deep down a spark of hope and strength waited to be heard.

There is no ending to this story, rather the unfolding of physical loss and the gradual acceptance of a reality that grows in the human heart over time. It is both the rot and perfume of life; sweet and sour, surface and deep, mine and maybe yours...a teacher with a lesson plan of patience and faith. I write these words decades later.

Much Too Busy (1986-1995)

I refused to admit there was a medical explanation for my initial loss of balance. My days were fully scheduled with family and teaching obligations. My sons and husband needed me, my students expected me to always be in school, and I felt much too young to have a serious physical problem. Being ill was not an option, and I even considered it a luxury to see a physician. No time. Besides, there were family vacations and weekend trips to plan.

I believed that my loss of balance was related to my changing hormones and would soon fade. I saw a neurologist every few months for a seizure disorder that I had since puberty, years prior to my ataxia diagnosis. All of my past symptoms were controlled with medication, and I simply required periodic blood tests followed by a physician check-up. The doctors always checked my reflexes and monitored my mobility, but never suggested further tests, and I never requested any. The lab test results were always good, so I convinced myself that, in general, everything was fine. That was my logic. Everyone assumed that my declining mobility was due to my medications. I accepted this as a satisfactory explanation. Once a doctor blurted out, "I bet you'll be in a wheelchair by the time you reach forty." I could never imagine that, and since he had no proof, I quickly ignored his comment. I have since learned that his comment was unnecessary since I started using a cane at age fifty-five.

Every change that occurred in the next few years, took place very slowly. I suffered quietly with each body breakdown. I knew something was happening. Most people did not notice and I became an expert at giving a logical explanation. I also became a pro at using whatever available assistance was nearby: walls, counters, furniture, even trees and bushes. I always grabbed the hands of my young sons and they never questioned my motherly gestures. Once our family visited a rocky beach and I had great difficulty walking. My four-year old son's hand became my support. At school, the students became great "little canes." I became skilled at hiding my challenges.

As the years passed, my limitations increased, but I continued to deny I had a problem. I assumed everything would fade with time. I sincerely believed that it was a temporary condition, and I possessed a body that would never be impaired in any way. Disabilities happened to other people; people in books or on television—never me. I was in my prime. I had a family, a home, a career. I had things to do. I was much too busy.

My Side Path into Darkness

Our bodies will teach us more than we can imagine, if only we will listen.

Mark Gerzon

Nine years after my initial tumble my body breakdown was happening more often. I suffered from all social stigmas associated with having a disability. I was convinced that the silent stares from others were harsh and critical. My fear of being judged was so intense that I could not believe their looks were of genuine concern. It felt as if a mysterious reality had taken over my body and mind. I was ashamed of my body and felt too different from most people. I allowed my shame and fears to seriously affect me. During that time my struggles involved both inner and outer breakdown. My life was over…my treasured body has failed. I wasn't certain if my handicap was more physical or emotional. Every day was a deeper journey into Darkness.

By the time I reached my forties, I had lost many motor abilities. I couldn't jump, skip, hop, or walk a straight line. I limited my social calendar. I felt I was a burden to be with—my disability was an inconvenience for my friends and an obstacle. In addition to physical loss, I lost inner strength and confidence. I lost my smile. This began my "I-Can't" phase. I can't run, I can't hike, I can't dance—the list was endless and growing.

One day as I circulated and stumbled through my second grade classroom a student innocently asked, "Why do you walk like that?" I responded in my usual manner, "Because I was in a car accident and hurt my legs." The truth was that I felt embarrassed that a seven-year-old child had noticed my sloppy gait. Even then I refused to admit my disability. I hid behind a lie. This felt like the safer and more acceptable route.

Whenever I needed to get into the car to drive, I grabbed the steering wheel for added support. My coordination and balance had failed. Ramps rather than stairs became necessary or, if I had stairs, I needed a two-sided banister. The worst and most painful aspect of this physical change was that no-one else had these challenges. I felt all alone. Self-pity consumed me. I chose to suffer in silence. I could not articulate what was happening to my body. Instead, I chose the path of denial. My denial and fears were toxic.

Despite the obvious erosion of my body, a deep inner voice struggled to be heard. It would be years before I recognized the cries. It was as if my bones were infused with an inner hope that refused to surrender—a joy beyond what I knew.

I still had many roads to travel. I still needed to be diagnosed. I still needed to find level ground.

Finding Level Ground

2

The Diagnosis

A Gray Day

Habitually I looked for flatter and flatter surfaces to walk on, yet I fell often. I used heating pads and ice packs on a daily basis to soothe the bone pain. If that didn't work, I turned towards ibuprofen™ or pain meds. But as the weeks unfolded, I knew I needed to face the medical facts—the painful and terrifying truth. I was only in my early forties, and for nine years had refused to hear medical proof of my condition. It was not easy. The thought of being flawed frightened me. Finally, exhausted by my own attempts of trying to remedy my situation, I scheduled the MRI.

After a fifty mile commute and a tiring day of teaching, I walked into the neurologist's office for the results. The doctor entered the examination room and put the test pictures in clear view. He projected no welcoming energy. All business.

"According to your brain images, the MRI shows significant loss in the cerebellum. The cerebellum is the region of the brain that controls motor activity." He pointed it out on the screen. "It's progressive. It's a form of ataxia termed cerebellar ataxia. At this time, there is no cure."

I was overwhelmed by the words *no cure* but refused to accept such a permanent, indelible fact. I had always believed otherwise—if something could not be proven, it was merely speculation and temporary. *Was I wrong? Was he telling me otherwise—that it was certainly final?* I couldn't think straight.

"Are there exercises I can do to reverse this?" I asked with desperation and a degree of hope. I wanted a magic solution. I dismissed the medical facts. "No", he continued, "Once brain tissue is lost, it cannot regenerate. People will assume you're drunk." He snickered and chuckled as he delivered his message.

BAM! I felt punched, slammed in a deep, dark, lonely, unfamiliar, and extremely vulnerable place. I failed to share the doctor's humor. At that moment, all I wanted to do was hide. I needed to be alone. I was scared, confused, and totally devastated. I had to escape from this nightmare. I left his office but what I really wanted was to find the door marked "Exit". *Get me out of here.* Instead, I walked through a door that had no exit. I entered my future.

The diagnosis uncovered much more than medical facts. It unleashed a multitude of fears, an assembly of shame, guilt, self-pity, and ultimately, feelings of separation and loneliness. Ever since childhood, I had felt my power emerged from the ability to manage or control my external environment—including my body. Now that was gone. Worse, I did not want to think about the impact of the diagnosis. It was a truth I didn't want to hear. I didn't expect it and I didn't want it.

I walked out into the grayness of the day. I wanted to get home, curl into a tight ball, and just disappear. I thought if I could hide the distressing diagnosis, it would just vanish—Poof! I reasoned that the further away I crawled, the better I'd feel. My world was now dark…confusion took root, spread deep into my being and my victim-self assumed the lead. Life would never be the same, Soon I collapsed to sleep.

The next day I awoke and quickly buried myself in the details of everyday life. It seemed safe at the time.

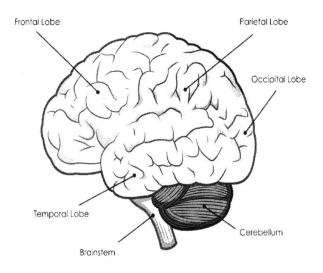

Cerebellum affects motor function

Finding Level Ground

The Guest House

This being human is a guest house.
Every morning a new arrival.
A joy, a depression, a meanness,
some momentary awareness comes
as an unexpected visitor.
Welcome and entertain them all!
Even if they are a crowd of sorrows,
who violently sweep your house
empty of its furniture,
still, treat each guest honorably.
He may be clearing you out
for some new delight.
The dark thought, the shame, the malice.
meet them at the door laughing and invite them in.
Be grateful for whatever comes.
because each has been sent
as a guide from beyond.

Jelaluddin Rumi, translated by Coleman Barks

My response to Rumi's poem — *The Guest House*

The Intruder

Before I could say "not welcome,"
an unwanted, uninvited intruder
entered and took control of my body.
He told me his name was Ataxia
and he brought messages from beyond —
He consumed my food,
robbed me of my gold,
rearranged my furniture, and
dimmed down the lights.
After years he remains, his message
still unclear. I continue to look for clues
but only find morsels of hope, hear
rhythms of the sea, whispers of wind,
and the quiet breath of my life's chapters.

3
The Raging Victim

Lost in Denial

What is not ex-pressed is de-pressed.
Mark Nepo

I could not forget the doctor's words: "You have cerebellar ataxia. It's progressive. There is no cure. People will assume you're drunk." His words haunted me for years. They played over and over in my mind like a scratch on a broken record. Accept it, my voice of reason whispered, but my fears took over. It was a constant battle between my fears and reason.

I had lost my footing in life. I felt these similar feelings of loss as a young seven year-old child when my mother died. I felt it again one year later after my grandfather passed away. Both deaths were unexpected. They had been my secure and familiar anchors of family love and acceptance. Suddenly they vanished. I felt there was nothing left in my life, only loss. Nothing could be done. After I received my ataxia diagnosis, these same empty feelings came roaring back. I hoped they were temporary. PLEASE, I pleaded.

Each stripped me of my inner strength and confidence. Ataxia affected so many areas in my life: personal relationships, friends, parties, health, recreation—a never-ending list of life. I was no longer the excited, ready-for-anything me. I was consumed by feelings of inadequacy and believed I was a burden to others. The fears kept multiplying. I allowed my physical disability to rob me of valuable human interaction. As my physical loss increased my self-pity grew.

I gradually began to read books and articles on the subject of loss. I felt there had to be a connection between my earlier loss of loved ones and my current physical deficiency. According to studies by Elisabeth Kubler-Ross, there are five stages–denial, anger, bargaining, depression, and acceptance. These unfold in no sequential order. For me, each stage revealed old wounds—low self-worth, self-deprecation, and shame. I made excuses for why I couldn't attend gatherings or join others. I blamed the bad weather or fabricated a prior commitment. I tried to hide the truth—even from myself. I could not and would not admit my cerebellar ataxia was real. I lived many years in denial of the fact I had a handicap. Even the word angered me.

My anger and depression increased as my sudden, spontaneous turns became dangerous. Often, they resulted in falls, bruises, and broken bones. I even had trouble walking the buffet lines, since it was difficult to use both hands when carrying anything. Fine and gross motor skills became a challenge. I lost my beautiful handwriting to the dreaded "chicken scratch." I was exhausted! My disability also uncovered a victim consciousness that I had never wanted. Poor me. I assumed I could blame, hide, and pray my way to better health. I did not want to research or attempt to understand the scientific explanations. Although I knew what the EEG, MRI, and all medical tests revealed, and the doctors said I had a type of ataxia that was progressive, I hid in denial, anger, and depression. I was afraid of research findings. I felt victimized.

I longed for the day I could feel the meaning of the word "acceptance." Acceptance was simply a foreign word.

How could I possibly accept this condition in my body? This shouldn't happen to me. I am much too young for something so awful. I continued to deny reality; I drowned myself in daily agendas. I relied on my teacher plan book and lists. That gave me some control. I ignored medical facts.

But what I didn't realize, I was on a journey — not of loss but of gain. I could not see that seeds had been planted and gardens would someday appear. "To everything there is a season…" I didn't feel I had any choices. That realization was yet to come.

The Placard

Shortly after I discovered I had ataxia, I requested a disabled placard from the DMV. I felt intensely angry with my physical condition and entitled to anything I could get. I was definitely eligible for a placard. Even though my ataxia was not obvious to most, my request seemed logical — if I'm labelled handicapped, I'm entitled to the benefits. When the blue plastic arrived, I felt ashamed and refused to admit I needed any assistance. The placard stayed hidden in my glove box for several years.

One February morning, years after the disastrous diagnosis, I headed off to my teaching job. Rain was predicted that day, and the air felt heavy and coated with impending dreariness. I arrived early, as usual, in order to secure a parking space close to the building. The ground would be wet by the time I clocked out later that afternoon. Walking on slick ground was now unsafe. My mobility had worsened, so running was no longer an option. I needed easy access to the school, so I quickly drove into the closest space designated for staff. Then my eyes targeted a closer parking space.

Finally, that gloomy February morning, I considered using my placard for the first time. The space marked "Disabled Parking Only" was ideal— wide open, close to the building, and I would not have far to walk in the expected rain. Logical. But an inner storm erupted. All kinds of fears raged within.

I am not handicapped….If I use it, people will know for sure….The students will find out….I'll be talked about, judged as flawed … I can't… The thought of attaching my identity to such a label was unacceptable. I was overwhelmed by the image of a person in a wheelchair. The thought of being different, or limited in any way, meant not being included by someone, and that fear was too much for me to bear. I wanted to be like everyone else. My reasoning always traced back to an intense sense of pride. I chose to suffer.

I inched my car into the handicap space. *No!* I backed out. *No!* I moved forward—then back. In-out-in-out. I hung, removed, and rehung the placard. On-off-on – I sobbed, and chose safety over fear for the first time. It was a deep belly cry, but I knew I finally made the right choice.

Gradually, as life continued and my mobility decreased, my decisions changed. I learned not to be so obsessed with my thoughts of what others may or may not think. Now my choices are made based on fact rather than fear or anger. My body taught me that safety is greater than a superficial pride.

I now believe that safety is much more important than fear. Today, years later, I no longer drive and do not have a glove box to hide my placard. Rather, I keep it with me at all times wherever I go. Today I am quick to remind the driver, "Look for the handicap space."
I speak with gratitude.

Perish the Pivot

As my cerebellum shrinks —
my body moves to a slower song,
perish the turns-twirls-twists,
perish the pivot.
My fast turns of past years
fade as days and nights fall
and dust settles, covers
my weary bones.
No longer adjusted to speed
I move to gradual beats
tuned instead to relaxed
rhythms of my soul.
My body moves me forward
like a bird with a broken wing
struggles to reach shelter,
like fish swimming against current
through rocky, torrential waters.
I move to a slower song,
perish the turns-twirls-twists
perish the pivot.

Victim Villanelle

Dark days define my gray-streaked room.
loss of balance signals falls
fears and doubts announce my doom.

The victim spreads—forever looms
throughout my veins, constructing walls
dark days define my grey-streaked room.

Blackened shadows dance of gloom
hopeless, heartless cackling calls—
fears and doubts announce my doom.

Seeds once planted will never bloom
wide fields have turned to narrow halls,
dark days define my gray-streaked room.

Stumbling, fading, worn-out womb
within my body a demon crawls
fears and doubts announce my doom.

My life now lost within a tomb
corridors of endless stalls—
dark days define my gray-streaked room.
fears and doubts announce my doom.

Finding Level Ground

4

Facing the Truth

The Hike Beyond the Main Road

So much has been given to me. I have no time to ponder over that which has been denied.
Helen Keller

I travelled throughout the western coast of the United States in the summer of 2004. Although I knew it would be a physical challenge because of my ataxia, I elected to hike along the "Waterfall Highway" located in southern Oregon. The travel brochure identified this 2.5 mile hike as "easy" and "handicap accessible." Laced with varieties of ferns, plants, and shady trees, this man-made compacted dirt trail had stone stairs and frequent handrails to provide safe access. Ordinarily, I resented the word *handicap*, however the opportunity to experience natural settings beyond my normal car passenger-view both thrilled and motivated me. Little did I realize this hike would provide much more than what the pamphlet described.

With a sturdy walking stick, I began to safely move along the path, and with each step my senses came alive. The songs of birds, nature's smell of green, and vibrant colors soon dominated the landscape and erased the harsh city sounds that had become too familiar. As I approached Toketee Falls, the sound of the water crashing against rocks, grew louder and enticed me. I met a woman as she made her return from the Falls and we began to chat. I gravitated to her welcoming smile and accepting mannerisms. Her words were not important, rather, her approach impressed me. As we communicated, I no longer felt separated from others—as if a heavy weight had been removed. I felt "normal."

During the past several years I buried the pain of separation deep within. On that hike my pain slowly began to surface and fade. As we talked, I finally recognized and accepted this. My heart beamed inclusion, and my footsteps moved to the tune of inner joy—a long unexpected joy.

My anticipation grew as I neared Toketee Falls; I felt the spray on my skin, heard the power of water hitting rock, and allowed my surroundings to rush through me. I finally connected with raw beauty, history, and the earth.

As sunlight faded, it was time to hike back to the main road. Even though walking downhill is strenuous with my ataxia, I felt pride and joy. My happiness overshadowed all my previous concerns about limitations with mobility. The thought *I can't* became *I can.*

Prior to this hike I believed my life was dictated by physical loss, and that I could never again experience life's natural beauty. Self-pity. Victim consciousness. During that hike my attitude towards disability shifted.

I reached for the handrails as I hiked back to the main road. A breathtaking sunset was predicted. I am grateful I didn't miss it.

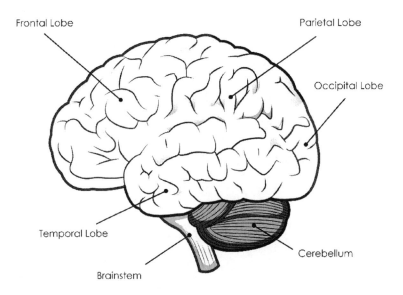

The Hike to Inclusion

Beyond the main road I travel —
Accompanied by scents of wet earth
delighted to breathe in
these earthly treasures.

With walking stick in hand
love of nature in my heart
and proud determination
by my side,
I begin my hike
on the waterfall trail
of lacy ferns and forest sounds.

No longer separate,
no longer fearful,
I partner with summer sun,
whispering wind,
and others on the path
I become a piece of the landscape.

Stone handrails and compacted
trails provide safe access
as I look in every direction—
anxious to finally see
the inside of this land,
excited to feel the water's mist
on my skin,

Overjoyed
to be able.

Value of Visibility

We are all just walking each other Home.
Ram Dass

I visited a secluded southern California beach in my thirties. It was an ideal time for a family outing. The warm June breezes welcomed us as we made our way across the rocky sands through a grove of palm trees to a semi-private spot. The harsh city sounds and crowds of people had faded. Instead, I heard the waves gently splash to shore. My view of the ocean was unobstructed, and I could see the water as it glistened on the rocks. It was time to relax.

As I soaked in the day and stared out at the distant ocean, I noticed a man lying on a yellow surfboard. He moved in rhythmic strokes; up and down, bobbing on his belly with the movement of the sea. Pure joy. I watched him for a long time until he finally rode the board to shore. When he stood, I was stunned. He had only one leg. Not long afterward, to my amazement, another man arrived on the beach. He was in a wheelchair with a boogie board in his lap. After his friend pushed the chair close to the shoreline, this man, having no legs, slid from his wheelchair onto his Styrofoam throne and paddled out to sea. I watched him play for a long time in the surf.

This took place many years before I learned that I would someday be afflicted with cerebellar ataxia. I was unexposed, at the time, to the many people that daily cope with body challenges. I never imagined that someday I'd have a similar struggle. Now I believe there was a reason I was on that beach that particular day. I didn't realize until years later what true human courage was. I received much more than a nice tan that day.

I am forever grateful I was on that beach that day. I share it as a reminder of the gift of every ability. I know this memory was locked in my inner depths and later revealed to me as an example of human possibility and determination. The why and how are not important. It taught me the value of joy, pride, and inner strength. It encouraged me to never be defeated by physical limitation, or by the words *I can't*. It instilled in me the necessity to keep moving like the waves, keep singing my way back to shore.

Years after my diagnosis, I met a man at the local fitness club. He recently underwent a serious operation, and lost motor function, however, his attitude was cheerful and positive. We spoke at length about the benefits of exercise for overall health, and we both agreed that all types of physical exertion must be kept up on a daily basis. He was a regular gym member.

Although this man had mobility issues, he walked to the club every day. He did this both for himself, and for the benefit of others to see. "You never know who will be watching you," he told me with confidence. "Other people need to see there is always hope; always be visible." He continued to explain how he had unknowingly been walking by the window of his neighbors who had a son with a similar disability. Their son had watched the man for years. One day they came outside to express their gratitude because their son now felt motivated to also walk. I can still hear his words: "Get out. Be visible. You never know who will see you."

Recently I travelled to the Grand Canyon. It is a majestic area, a place of natural beauty, and a popular site where many world-wide visitors swarm. The tour bus I travelled on offered me accessibility, and we stopped at many level lookouts. I was able to use my walker for easier mobility. Most of the people on the bus did not need such assistance. At a stopping-point along the tour route, a couple approached me to thank me for being there. They said they had watched me with my walker and it reminded them how grateful they were with their own physical abilities. They said they felt inspired by my courage and efforts. "Yes", I agreed. I smiled and silently gave thanks. Finally, after years of self-doubt, shame, and unneeded seclusion I joined in on life. I felt grateful for the easy access to do so, and I felt deep gratitude for all the brave and determined people who helped provide the significant ADA legislation opportunities we have today.

The opinion of others can be a powerful motivation. I have witnessed this as both receiver and giver. For too long I feared that people judged and pitied me for my physical limitations. I now believe there is a difference between pity and compassion. I have felt both. Pity feels like I'm being devalued. Compassion feels like a warm hug. I prefer warm hugs.

I continue to seek level ground.

Against Whitewater

With yellow board
and belly-down,
he rode far out
to sea. Led
by waves, wind
and sky—his arms
paddled against
white water, against
ocean currents,
away from critical
and glaring eyes.
He moved with grace,
never standing
danced the ocean's
rhythm.

We watched him
float to the horizon,
befriend the clouds,
the sun, the salty
world that whispered
his strength.

We watched
as the final wave
gently carried him
to the rocky shore,
wrapped him in
mist and foam.

And as he emerged
We watched him lift
his brown legless body
with pride and joy
with a silent knowing.

The Final Bell Rings

In June 2005, I packed my briefcase, left the room in order and locked the elementary classroom door for the final time. I took the memories of a twenty year teaching career with me. For the past several years, I knew my ataxia had progressed. During this last school year, I was absent too many days due to constant illness. Weakness and fear of falling occupied my thoughts and took over my body. It became difficult to walk across the schoolyard or make my way to the office. I could no longer take advantage of my social time. Even the lunchroom was off limits. I retired at age 55 with a disability. Regardless of how hard I tried to hide my physical condition, I could no longer deny the truth.

Normally, the last day of any school year is a time for celebration, but that day was different. It marked the end of an era and the beginning of new unchartered territory. The thought of not having to get up early, or do nightly paperwork, or commute a long distance to work thrilled me. However, my admission of being disabled terrified me. *Was this an ending or a beginning?*

The time had come to retire and re-think. During the past years, many students came and went. During my career as a teacher, I always taught my students to understand and locate the beginning, middle, and end of a story. I explained that there will be new developments along the way. There will always be turns along the paths. Now the time arrived to learn this firsthand as a student. My lessons had just begun. In all that time of instruction, I now believe the most important student was me. The teacher happened to be my body, and my body now instructed me to slow down.

Until this time, I had lived a pre-planned existence and measured my days and thoughts by how efficiently things went. The clock and the calendar were central to my decisions. I calculated every lesson and activity to the minute. I took pride in my organizational abilities. When that final bell rang, I entered a new "time zone" based on a much deeper clock, an internal clock, a clock that can't be measured, seen or heard.

I began to read and contemplate the stages of loss and possible alternative methods of healing my inner turmoil. *Was I alone? Is there anyone else who feels this way?* Since there is no definite cure for cerebellar ataxia, I felt it necessary to investigate other ways to find relief from the trials of body breakdown. The term *victim* kept reappearing. I wanted to learn more…

Gradually I realized how victim-consciousness limited my thoughts, experiences and kept me away from people. The idea that I had no control over the events that happened to me became false. I knew that type of thinking could be changed. Living with cerebellar ataxia is both difficult and demanding. It requires an enormous amount of patience and tremendous self-love and self-care. There is no time for victim-consciousness.

However, there needs to be a distinction between physical and emotional healing and I needed to find my *inner warrior.* I needed time to listen, time to be receptive, time to re-define and re-adjust my thoughts, and time to think beyond myself. I hope this time and awareness will come to you, and come before the final bell rings.

Part II

More Than My Drama

Finding Level Ground

5
Perspectives Change

Loosening the Ground

The quieter you become the more you can hear.
Ram Dass

In the spring of 2005 I prepared for a major
life-shift. My body demanded rest without
schedules or forced plans, and I felt compelled to
listen to my body. It was time to honor my physical
needs, learn to accept I had ataxia. My lengthy
history of living with losing balance and falls
contributed to this decision. My ongoing denial had
become repetitive and boring, and I grew tired of
complaining. Besides, I missed my smile and
dimples. Even though I didn't enjoy facing the
truth, I had to accept an early retirement. I initiated
the necessary paperwork required by my employer.
Six months later, I was officially categorized as a
disabled retiree.

Within months my external and internal life
changed. I moved from the city with freeways and
long commutes to the country, to a tranquil, calm,

and peaceful lifestyle. I was finally able to sleep without the interruption of alarm clocks or deadlines. I walked through forests where I spotted birds flit from branch to bush. I heard sounds of water hit rock. I smelled roses, fresh mint, and skunks. I felt rain as it fell to earth. Beauty. Struggle. I took baby steps towards the acceptance of my disability. It was as if I had emerged from a dark, haunting forest into a small patch of light and fresh air. I needed to finally breathe.

During the following spring, I planted a vegetable and flower garden. Not all of the seeds sprouted. It was much like life. I observed the earthworms loosen soil to promote the blooms. I sensed rays of sunlight nourish the plants and observed the rain soak into the roots. As I watched the plants develop I wondered about my own life cycle. *Did my ataxia make me less able to come into full bloom?* My garden became a compassionate teacher, trustworthy partner, and guide. I identified with both the beauty and the challenges of life. I absorbed a world of opposites and no longer felt alone.

I also started an inner garden including daily reading and studied different philosophies. Perspectives changed. I spent hours in contemplation, and my interest in writing uncovered hidden energies. Most of my dramas no longer felt important—or necessary. I had become more than my stories, but I needed to cross additional hurdles.

I was grateful for my growing awareness, but I knew I had bigger steps ahead of me. Dealing with my vanity and controlling a strong sense of pride topped the list. I still refused to use my multiple canes. I kept them hidden, and the walker was out of the question. Even though my body had taught me a great deal, I needed to listen on a deeper level. Many medical and emotional obstacles remained on my path. Like the earthworm that loosened the soil for my outdoor garden, I had to loosen the soil of my inner life in order to enrich the quality of my days.

Vanity From an Early Age

Change the Way You Look at Things, and the Things you look at Change

Wayne Dyer

My focus on outward appearances started as a young girl. I was so excited when Grandma took my brother and me to a local park with stables and horses to rent. I was only eight and I wanted the most beautiful horse because that's what they rode in story books. The only horses I ever saw were in books or the wooden ones at amusement parks. The day we arrived at the stable I felt thrilled, and chose the white horse with long legs and a long tail. She was the best looking, just like a real cowgirl rides. This white beauty stood alone among the rest of the horses and looked a bit nervous. I wondered if she was new to the stable and afraid, but I was determined to have her. I was eight years old, and did not know what might happen.

The stable owner helped me onto the saddle and instructed me on how to ride. "Give her a good kick and she will start moving," he explained. At first the horse responded, but after a few kicks, she reared up, and I was thrown to the ground. The horse was confused with her new surroundings, and I was unaware that she was young and frisky and not used to beginning riders. As I lay in the dirt crying, the stable owner insisted, "If you don't get back on a horse, you will always be afraid of horses." He wanted me to choose an older, slower one. After I stopped crying I listened to his reason, and chose a less glamorous looking, but more established horse. I re-mounted, and from that point on the ride was fun. I learned that I can conquer my fears, and become self-confident. I learned to look beyond surface appearances. I learned those lessons, but often failed to apply them.

Over the next several decades, I bought into the cultural myth that beauty can be attained if I followed popular trends. I spent hours ironing my curls to look like the models seen in magazines and on T.V. I spent both time and hard-earned money shopping for clothes and cosmetics, yet rarely used them. I even worried about the color of my socks being fashionably correct. As a teenage girl, I hid a pair of orthopedic shoes in the bushes so that my friends wouldn't see and judge me. I concentrated on my outward appearance. Looks were everything.

My concern for outward appearances gradually changed after I received my diagnosis. The emphasis on inner growth took over all of my energies. I realized, fall after fall, my vanity held me back.

Time to undo the myth— let go of superficial ideas, and take a more loving, meaningful, heartfelt, and genuine approach. My past defines who I am, and how I cope with life. I carry these memories in my heart. Despite the fact that my body is physically breaking down, I treasure my inner strengths of resilience, courage, and fortitude. They are deeply embedded within. I can understand how my outdated belief in vanity blocked any positive self-growth. Vanity is a dead end. I need to walk a different path.

Vanity Surrenders: The Cane

I was in my late 50's and lived with denial and anger for nearly 25 years. I finally admitted this. Well-meaning people frequently asked, "Why don't you use a cane?" This only served to increase and fuel my anger. "I will not use a cane," I told everyone who brought up the subject, "I am much too young, I'm fine, no worries." The cane threatened my vanity. This included everything from body image such as dress size, hair length, color, make-up, to how I spoke, moved, and who my friends were—basically everything material and superficial. I both treasured and accepted my vanity. I had an image of physical beauty, and thought I knew what that meant. I had learned about it growing up. I struggled to maintain it, and in my eyes, a cane threatened that beauty, and my independence.

On the night of the 2008 summer solstice I awoke from a sound sleep and quickly stood. But when I tried to walk, my body refused to move quickly. Instead, I fell to the floor, and landed hard on my wrist. I was overwhelmed with an intense pain. When I tried to push myself up, I had no strength. My forearm quickly turned black. My loud groans travelled throughout the house, cutting the night air.

Within minutes my husband drove me to the hospital. I braced my left wrist with my right hand for that entire drive. Every little bump on the road was magnified; the trip took forever. My hand was completely swollen; the pain unbearable. By the time I arrived at the emergency room, the bones showed through my skin.

After the nurse helped me onto a bed she told me, "Your rings are a problem. We need to cut them off. The circulation is being compromised. She proceeded to use wire cutters to remove them." *How could I have done this to myself,* I thought in my familiar, scolding voice. Six hours later I was wheeled into surgery. All I could think was *please let this be fixed. I've learned my lesson. I'll use a cane. Please let this be fixed.*

On that night of the summer solstice everything changed. Surgery fixed both my body and my mental attitude. For six long and restrictive weeks I lay in bed, thinking, re-evaluating, and eventually transforming my life-long opinion of myself. It was time to relinquish vanity for safety. I did not like my dependence on Tylenol™ every four hours, Ibuprofen™ every eight, ice packs, heating pads, and heightened pillows for comfort. My denial was too painful, and no longer served me. Vanity was certainly not an asset.

As soon as I could leave the house, I went to a local pharmacy and purchased a cane. I compromised and bought a decorative cane, something fashionable. The green and magenta colors even matched my bedroom walls and door molding. More important, the cane became my new and faithful assistant. It became my friend.

The night of the 2008 summer solstice marked the beginning of a new season: time for renewed thinking and a shift to inner growth. It became my personal anniversary of self-acceptance, planting seeds of freedom. This anniversary was also the arrival of a new, unexpected friend disguised as a cane.

Another Break

Be patient toward all that is unsolved in your heart, try to love the questions themselves like locked rooms.

Ranier Marie Rilke

During my early 60's I kept as mobile as possible with activities both in and out of the house. My cane was my reliable, faithful, and constant companion. Home and garden were my special sanctuaries, and it was always a treat to spend days with family and friends. I travelled whenever possible and looked forward to trips to new and exciting places. A vacation to Mexico, swimming with dolphins and touring the ancient ruins, was unforgettable. I volunteered with a local environmental group for seven years, headed an annual fundraiser and serving at their various functions. I was active with writing groups and took many exercise classes at the local fitness center. I did what I physically could and especially enjoyed occasional kayaking trips on warm sunny days. The Central California coast is a nature lover's paradise, but my list of outdoor activities dwindled, as did my body.

One day I needed to take a large bedspread to the local cleaners. I knew it would be too bulky to transfer into my car. I was still capable of driving, but it had become too difficult to walk while carrying anything big. I decided to transport the huge spread on a walker, concealed in the garage, to the backseat of my Saturn. I kept the walker hidden because I refused to admit I needed it. *How would I look?* Vanity constantly haunted me! What I didn't understand was this device has wheels and requires that the brakes be locked when not moving, otherwise the walker will roll away. Mindlessly, I leaned into my car—put the bedspread on the seat, accidentally kicked the wheels, and the walker rolled down the driveway. I lost my balance and fell hard on the concrete. **Smack.** I passed out and nobody was around to help. After I regained consciousness, I pulled myself half-way up, shimmied into the house on my knees, got an icepack, and called my friend for further assistance.

My leg continued to swell, and that began the broken leg chapter. I was forced into bed and a wheelchair for six long weeks of rest, ice packs, heating pads, and regular Ibuprofen™. No more going out by myself, no more quick trips to the store, no more exercise, no more sudden movements. This was my second broken bone, and I wanted it to be my last. Time to heal and contemplate my life. Again. For the next several weeks I learned the benefits of stillness and the hidden beauty buried deep within the quiet, gentler regions of my human heart. I knew I was being instructed from within, and I chose to listen.

At first I felt caged in my room, but after the initial shock and pain from the fall faded, I began to read and write on a regular basis. My attitudes shifted from my external appearance to deep inner feelings.

My reality slowly changed. Over time I felt like a welcome guest at my own table. I no longer heard the harsh, familiar surrounding noises. Instead, newer sounds entered my space; tones from the wind chimes played gentler notes, birds called to announce their presence, and the koi splashed as they played in the backyard pond. I felt breezes blow through the screens as they mixed with the sun's warmth. Scents both sweet and sour poured into my space. I began to dream in color.

Pain had a place. Pleasure had a place. Up was down. Black was white. Leaves on the trees outside my window filled the branches. My grief morphed into joy, and I was doing nothing—nothing active.

My broken bone allowed me the long-overdue, needed break from the schedules I had self-imposed. Again, I questioned the benefits of only seeing and judging what I heard or saw on the surface of life. Vanity. I wanted to see beyond the one-way mirrors I had grown accustomed to. There had to be a deeper meaning.

Vanity Surrenders: The Walker

For the next few years, the cane had become a necessary, trusted friend. I realized it provided extra support. As time unfolded, I stopped worrying about others' opinions or judgments of how I looked. Instead, my dependence on the cane's stability and safety were more important. Soon, I had a collection of canes to fit each mobility need. All of the self-imposed social labels no longer mattered. My self-worth was strong, or so I thought...

One day I returned from a water aquatics class, opened the front door and saw a walker. A friend gave it to me as a gift, but rather than showing appreciation, I yelled in a very nasty voice, "Get that out of here!" Pure fear disguised as anger. The walker represented a new threat to my identity. Again, I was overwhelmed and refused to look or consider the benefits it provided. Instead, I reacted, wanted the four-wheeled device gone from my sight and out of mind. Again, the thought of being a disabled person was too much to bear.

As the season changed, and time moved forward as it always does, my body also moved in a new direction. My recent physical breakdown made me think that it might finally be time to surrender once again. By then reliance on complete steadiness of the cane had grown difficult—its support was not enough. I knew I needed to bring the walker out of storage. I didn't want to be controlled by outside opinions. Safety was primary.

At first I could not openly admit that I needed this assistance. I believed it was not normal for anybody my age to use a walker. My view of a person attached to a wheel chair haunted me. But over time, with added use and continued awareness, my attitude changed. I discovered that, in addition to added stability, the walker provided confidence and freedom to move in independent and less restrictive ways. I could join friends for walks or navigate on my own. It was much easier than the cane.

I believe my negative self-perceptions have melted away. During the past several years my mobility has decreased. Too often that translated to a desperate neediness in relationships. Today, the walker allows me the freedom to navigate the world with greater independence. I no longer need assistance for minor tasks. I feel more self-sufficient. I love my mutual, healthy, and sacred connection with others. I can go more places with friends. We can travel together. We can go on walks together. We can make memories together. I can share the good times rather than just sitting home feeling sorry for myself.

The transition from cane to walker has become part of my history. Today, I accept all help with gratitude and joy. I use the walker for assistance, and I know I made the right choice to surrender my vanity.

I continue to seek level ground.

The Perfect Pause

After the pain of the fall faded,
stillness swept through my days
and I resigned myself to rest.
No more schedules and lists.
Gone was the ticking of the clock

replaced by winds whispering
welcome, restored by the hugs
and warmth of the sun.
Timeless reminders hung

in the silence of both sweet
and sour days. I journeyed
deep within—past all doubts
and fear. As the birds sang,

I relaxed on broken bones hoping,
praying, and silently knowing
night stars sprinkle healing,
skies deliver change.

Finding Level Ground

6
Untying the Knots

A Glimmer of Hope

Be miserable or motivate yourself. Whatever has to be done it's always your choice.

Wayne Dyer

I spent many days alone because I felt alienated from others. Because I could not walk long distances, hike, or dance, I felt that nobody wanted to be with me. I felt like "a downer," and had lost control over my destiny due to my condition. For years I convinced myself life was over. *"How can I ever experience the joy that others speak of? My body is flawed. I have no influence over my life's outcomes. It's a done deal. I have no control. Poor, poor me."* My role as a victim was repetitive and boring, and I wanted to change my attitudes and reverse my negative beliefs. These toxic thoughts consumed me.

One sunny day in the spring of 2011, I went outside to soak in the golden light. I enjoyed times of inner peace, relaxation, and gardening in my backyard. It became my happy place and special sanctuary for solitude and contemplation. I turned to motivational and inspirational reading whenever possible. The hopeful messages combined with sunlight always comforted me.

I had started to read about the effects of positive thoughts on brain function, and the more I read, the more I realized that choice was available to everyone—even me. I can choose to remain unhappy or change my outlook. My choice. My control. This notion intrigued me.

Wayne Dyer's book entitled "Change Your Thoughts, Change Your Life" had a great influence. It was if his words were directed towards me – *"…with everything that has happened to you, you can either feel sorry for yourself or treat what has happened as a gift. Everything is either an opportunity to grow or an obstacle to keep you from growing. You get to choose."* His words triggered powerful thoughts. I closed the book, both literally and figuratively, glanced up, and noticed the butterflies on the flowers next to my seat. They had been beside me the entire day. I breathed in a silent knowing and realized that I was part of something greater. I had a purpose.

That message has influenced my life and contributed to the reactions and decisions I face. The words remain as my glimmer of hope, embedded deep within my being. It was on that spring day in 2011 that I began to say goodbye to my victim-self and welcome to lasting joy.

The Gratitude Highway

May I see my own limits with compassion just as I view the limits of others.

Roshi Joan Halifax

My attitudes about people with disabilities have changed over time. Prior to my diagnosis I viewed anyone with a physical handicap as being completely set apart from me. I judged them as freaks of nature. As a child I felt confused when I witnessed anyone with a deformity. I believed the neighbor boy with the small head was from another planet; the woman in my great-grandma's rest home was just a victim in a wheelchair; and retarded kids were different and didn't deserve any kindness, because they wouldn't understand. These were my opinions for more than thirty-five years. And then life changed me.

When the neurologist delivered my diagnosis of cerebellar ataxia, he told me it was a chronic condition. No cure. I was both terrified and devastated, but since my symptoms were only mildly obvious I denied the diagnosis. I knew my body suffered from something, but in my mind the terms "handicapped" and "cripple" were unacceptable. My greatest challenge was the idea of being different, because different meant separate. I felt that a disability involved alienation from others — either you are rejected or accepted. I was ashamed of my limits in spite of my accomplishments. I watched movies about leper colonies and other isolated groups. I had been in homes and schools for those handicapped. I was consumed with fears. This was the knot I needed to untangle and accept.

It was not until I took the long, winding journey on "the gratitude highway" that my outlook changed. My understanding of the word "gratitude" developed from reading or hearing about it. Gratitude was something that happened for others, not me. I only used the term on certain holidays, mostly as part of a religious ritual. I knew how to speak about gratitude, but I never felt gratitude until I directly experienced the deeper meaning. As my physical body slowed down, my inner self sped up. I began to view the world from a new perspective; I started to untangle my prior judgments and pre-conceived notions. In time the knotted web of harsh and fixed beliefs softened, and new attitudes emerged. I consciously started to speak about my experiences in more positive ways. I started a gratitude journal, and began listing everything that I felt grateful for: my family and friends, home, career—everything I dreamed of and received. I learned to speak, think, and pray gratitude.

I finally started to smile. I began to again experience the beauty of nature and the changes in seasons. I felt the power of both the hot sun and cold rain. I noticed that my individual world, with all the various and changing sounds, colors, and smells around me, was the same for everyone. My outlooks changed. The handicapped body I originally believed as abnormal now belonged in this bigger perspective. I was no longer disconnected from everyone, and needed to re-interpret the word *disability*.

I recognize the value of sharing other people's life stories as well as my own. I reached out and learned there are more common feelings among people than I once thought. I was no different. I remembered occasions from years earlier—I tried to help a blind girl, but she pulled away from my hand. At the time, I interpreted her as an angry person. I finally understood her pain and why she resisted. I watched a woman with multiple sclerosis fall and refuse help. I felt her unspoken disappointment and frustration with her body, and I understood how much pride is connected to body struggle.

As I continued to practice gratitude, I shed unnecessary fears and realized that my life was greater than I once thought. I started to feel accepted and welcomed by others, and appreciated their kindness towards me. I began to understand the value of friendships, and every time I gave or received a smile or a hug, I was grateful.

I sincerely hope that as my ataxia progresses, my feeling of separateness continues to dissolve and my heart grows. I am grateful for this awareness and my journey on "the gratitude highway."

May kindness endure as we **all** find level ground.

Trail of Terror – Choice point

In the spring of 2009, I experienced a real scare. I was driving my car to be serviced and was in a hurry. As I quickly turned the corner, I made a wide turn and weaved into both right and left-hand turn-lanes. I continued to drive unaware of my wide turn. Immediately, a small white car came up behind me. It was about one foot from my rear bumper. I sped up, but the driver would not relent. I was confused by his aggressiveness, honks, and frequent hand gestures.

There were no red and blue lights on his vehicle so I kept driving. After one mile he lowered his visor with the reflective tape, and flashed those official colors typical of police. It was an unmarked car, and I immediately pulled over. A very tall man with a police badge approached my window. "Have you taken any medication?" he asked in a commanding and angry tone. "Just my prescribed pills," I answered, not realizing that was not the answer I should have given. Fortunately, I carried both my handicap placard and a doctor's letter in my glove box to help explain my physical condition. This officer never heard of ataxia and refused to listen to the medical explanation. I tried to explain that it was a neurological condition, but he didn't seem to care. He was angry. I was humiliated and very frightened.

Within a few minutes, an official police car pulled up, but I was fortunately and technically out of their city jurisdiction. The city officers took away my license, and wanted to arrest me on a DUI. They called for a third police car, a California sheriff from San Luis Obispo County that could make the arrest.

I was in shock. I had always obeyed laws and for years stressed the importance of rules in my classrooms. Now, everything was upside-down, inside-out, unreal and totally foreign. While the officers discussed my fate, I stared out into the rich, brown farm fields adjacent to my car window and waited. I thought about all the years I worried about what people thought of me and realized how senseless that was and how much my ideas had finally blossomed in mature and nourishing directions. I felt sorry for these officers lost in petty regulations and limited judgments. I knew they did not see past their rule books, could not breathe the freshness of the air, and were blind to the beautiful natural setting before us. I also knew they held a certain power. Fortunately, the third policeman understood reason. After they all spent an hour discussing my situation, Officer #3 returned my license that Officer #2 had taken from me. He told me that I was free to go.

Several weeks later, I received a letter from the Safety Division of the DMV. My license had been suspended until they could speak with me. The date for the meeting was scheduled in six weeks. No more driving. I felt as if I was in a nightmare. A radical transformation had been thrust upon me and I was not prepared to accept this life-changing experience. Weeks passed, and I met with the safety official. Because I had all the medical documentation to prove I was under good care, they allowed me to re-take a road test and keep my license. I decided to ensure passing the test and enrolled in refresher driving classes.

My license was renewed. In addition I was expected to carry an official DMV letter that acknowledged they were aware of my condition. Two weeks later I was pulled over once again on a different road for weaving. This time the officer was

very compassionate, however, I was deeply
concerned about my future as a driver. I started to
seriously re-think my choices in life. I thought about
the extent of my physical abilities and my safety. I
thought about my driving. After much
contemplation, I surrendered my license five years
later. I was scared when I knew I had to give up
driving. Driving signified a freedom and
independence that I did not want to surrender. I
had lived on my own scheduled time since age
sixteen. I went where I wanted, when I wanted.
Slowly, this freedom had slipped away. I would
need to depend on others, something I had never
done and was not comfortable doing. I would need
to ask for help, another radical and distasteful
thought. I also knew, despite all of my negative
thoughts, that patience was my best choice. Not
easy but right. It was obvious to everyone,
including me, that my mobility skills were affected.
I had to decide between convenience and my
physical safety. I had to remind myself: slow down,
give up unrealistic expectations, and accept
whatever happens. I needed to find my inner
warrior. I needed to give up driving. I needed to
surrender. I needed to make a healthy choice.

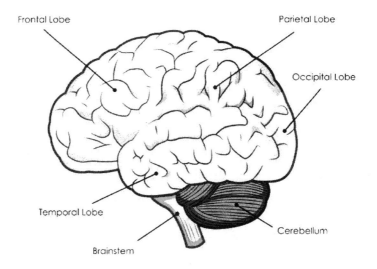

7
Healthy Choices

Asking for Help

Ask for help not because you're weak, but because you want to remain strong.

Les Brown

For years my choices revolved around what I believed was socially acceptable or best for everyone else. The needs of others' came before my own. As a young wife and mother, I commuted long distances to and from work. While this provided financial benefits for the family's welfare, I refused to acknowledge the stress it had on my body. When my disabled placard first arrived, I never used it, convinced that somebody else needed the space more. I limited my social activities, not wanting friends to feel obligated to help me. I hoped everyone liked and wanted to be with me. Above all else, I denied my limitations.

Central to my beliefs was the notion that outside help was unnecessary. In the beginning stages of my mobility loss, I refused to ask for help or to accept help of any kind. I refused to admit I needed any type of assistance. Even though medical facts stated otherwise, I rejected the benefits of a cane, walker, or wheelchair. If a person noticed that I could use a hand, I rejected their offer. In my mind, asking was an admission of being flawed, and a sign of a weak mind and body. Whenever people tried to lend support, I'd quickly say, "Thanks, but I can do it myself; I'm fine." Their compassion was misunderstood as unsolicited sympathy. Sympathy was for the weak. I failed to consider what was practical or what I needed. I adamantly told myself—*I'm too young to request assistance. That's for old people.* I had a classic case of denial, fear, and more fear. I was full of anger.

But as my ataxia progressed, it took more and more energy to conceal it, which exhausted me. Year after year, like a slow dripping faucet, my pride eroded my growth. I realized I needed to change my thoughts. I had to learn to accept and ask for help. Asking for help became an important part of my self-care and a healthy choice.

I recognized it was time to re-define my needs and realize the importance of safety—again. During my teaching years I requested teacher assistants from my school district to help with my class. I discovered they were invaluable, especially when I needed to take the students outside or get around quickly. By my mid-fifties, my needs had increased considerably.

When I chose to give up driving, I also gave up a great deal of independence and personal power. It was difficult to quit jumping in my car whenever I needed to go somewhere, yet it provided an invaluable opportunity to understand the value of asking for and receiving help. I had to learn to depend on others' schedules, including public shuttles, and I was challenged to accept timelines other than my own. Giving up driving ranks as one of my supreme healthy choices. The need for personal safety had become clear.

As the years unfolded so did a mindful and healthy decision-making process. This freed me to journey within, into unchartered regions. I had to lose my rigid definitions before I could grow into the type of person that I wanted to be. Time to accept the natural rhythms of life. My season for healthy choices had arrived.

Now my gratitude prevails, and I realize that, as I open myself, I also give the giver a chance to express kindness. Making healthy life choices has made me shift my thoughts from separate to a connected sense of self. My decisions have transformed from narrow, selfish, and fearful behaviors to more inclusive outlooks; from a limited world view to the bigger picture; from me to us; from weak to strong.

I continue to seek level ground.

Self-Talk

Do not let what you cannot do interfere with what you can do.
John Wooden

From the time of my ataxia diagnosis I was at a crossroads. As my body broke down, my inner conflicts increased. My successful career as a teacher ended at age fifty-five with a disability retirement. My falls had become frequent and the quality of my work suffered. Ten years later, I faced another life-changing decision. In March 2015 after thirty-five years of marriage I divorced and sold my home. The family memories were great, yet I was not happy. I was torn between chaos and my health. I refused to allow the limitations from my ataxia to prevent me from moving forward in positive directions. My external comforts became far less important than the desire for inner peace. My meditation practice had released self-doubts and fears that I thought I had previously addressed. Shame, confusion, and disappointment over my physical condition outweighed any positive thoughts. It was so deep and personal that I noticed I began conversations with an apology. "I'm sorry." Mostly all of my interactions included the words "I can't." It was time to reverse this habit. Time to re-

examine and cultivate my choice of words—
beginning with self-talk.

Automatic excuses for not joining group
activities dominated my self-talk. I convinced
myself "I'm too tired, too busy, or I can't do that. I
wouldn't be fun." The list of everything I couldn't
do had overshadowed my abilities. I can't hike, I
can't walk in the sand, I can't go to that because of
bleacher seating, I can't, I can't...." I became my
own worst enemy. My self-talk was harsh and self-
defeating, and as social interactions dwindled my
self-esteem grew worse. As the loneliness grew
unbearable, I wanted different behaviors; and
intended to reverse these ways. Time to let go of
fears and trust that people accepted me for who I
was. I wanted to stop clinging to the thought that
others judged or pitied me. I discovered that the
judge I heard was none other than myself.

As the years unfolded, I tried to make
healthy choices and not live life as a victim of
circumstance. Instead, I desired a life I could be
proud of. I moved to the California Central Coast
in 2006, after I retired from teaching. For the first
several months, my time was devoted to inner

work—reading and listening to self-help tapes. One day when I was feeling victimized by my health, I read a book by Carl Jung. I still remember the line that stated, "I am not what has happened to me. I am what I choose to become." When I read those words, they resonated strongly, and realized I had forgotten my inner strength and prior convictions. His words motivated me.

I posted the words "I can, I will…" on my refrigerator, mirrors—throughout my living space. During that period I became interested in environmental issues, and headed a successful seven-year long fundraising committee for a local wildlife organization. I joined writing groups. I joined exercise activities. I expanded my friendships. I felt good about life and my self-talk slowly improved.

Today, my nightstand is filled with journals of positive quotes and affirmations. I repeat them to myself daily, and change any self-degrading comments after re-reading my journal entries. For me, writing is an effective tool to help clarify my thoughts, choices, and use of words. It reminds me to use positive language, and a gentle work in self-control. Having positive self-talk and attention to what I can do is the key. Awareness and recognition of my abilities help. It is better than complaining about my limitations. The saying that everything "is as it is" has become my mantra. This attitude of acceptance is my gentle gateway to joy and higher consciousness. It is my intimate, ongoing conversation with the universe; as I continue to search for level ground.

Moving Slowly

Our bodies will teach us more than we can imagine, if only we will listen.

Mark Gerzon from *Listening to Midlife*

I had defined myself as "the queen of falling." This self-degrading labelling had to stop. I wanted to instill compassion into my everyday thoughts, and knew I needed to move at a slower pace. The challenges were not to deny my limitations, but to accept them, not to struggle against the current. Accept what is and work with it.

Ataxia and moving quickly do not mix. Everyday my challenges increase: I fall and bruise easily. Simple tasks like personal hygiene, grocery shopping, or carrying laundry need careful planning. When indoors, I depend on walls, counters, and furniture to be my balancing supports and they must be in comfortable distance for easy reach. When outside, the trees, bushes, or whatever I find nearby become my helpers. My footsteps are carefully pre-planned as it is important to accomplish chores efficiently and in a timely manner.

As I lost cerebellar tissue, sudden movements became impossible. Carrying dishes requires slow, careful hands and feet. On one occasion, I quickly pulled a casserole dish from the oven and lost my balance. My dinner landed on the floor. I stopped offering tea or coffee to guests because of the danger of burning myself or them with hot liquid. A bath or shower became time-consuming as the slightest turn on slippery surfaces could end in disaster. My fear of falling remains great, and common everyday abilities are now precious memories. When someone asks me to "hurry," I have to remind them that "I don't do hurry." In the past several years I have experienced emergency surgery, broken bones, bruised ribs—none of which I want to repeat.

Besides the physical discomfort, each incident magnified my victim-self. I was frustrated, became discouraged with my body, and had little patience. When I chose to live on my own in 2015, and care for myself with little assistance, my fear of falls intensified. I tried to adapt my habits, to be slow and cautious. One night I awoke and moved too quickly. Down I went. Unlike years prior, no one was around to hear me. Thankfully, nothing broke.

The message: "yet slower." The learning curve is endless. The acceptance of my slow body movements did not occur overnight.

For years I made decisions without thought of the consequences. I suffered until I tried to learn the lessons from my stories: *Perhaps my body is telling me to slow down. I have nowhere to go, no one to hurry for, no schedules, certainly no speed-limit signs. I don't want any more breaks. Maybe I should listen.* My body was teaching me the importance of patience and self-compassion. It was time to pay attention.

In the words of Anais Nin, "And the day came when the risk to remain in a tight bud was more painful than the risk it took to blossom." Implementing this lesson has become a healthy, rewarding, and wise choice. I now understand it is better to live at a realistic pace than to turn away from life. My weekly schedule is filled with activities, friends, and quality alone-time. I learned to work "with rather than against." I'm forever grateful that I listened to the message from my body—Slow Down.

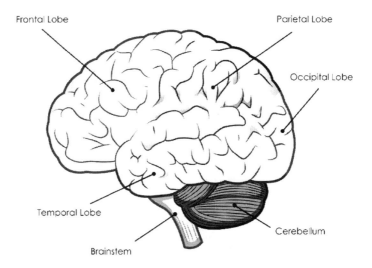

Finding Level Ground

The Clouds Keep Moving

Despite dire forecasts,
the clouds keep moving —
colors boast beauty from
dawn to dusk.

I see parades of people crying war
I hear the rise of joy, smell streaks
of pain as I watch beneath umbrellas
of floating clouds.

and despite dire forecasts,
our bodies keep moving —
a timeless, birthless,
deathless dance

parades of earth rhythms
once hard and fast, now
slow... slow... slow, yet soft
as I gently glide towards

a destination unknown.
All the while, the universal heartbeat
remains interwoven,
intertwined as the clouds keep moving

Finding Level Ground

Part III

Healing

Acceptance

Finding Level Ground

8
Open the Toolbox

Exercise – A Key Ingredient

Explore new worlds within you, open new channels of thought
Henry David Thoreau

The time had come to change my lifestyle. My life as a busy mom and teacher centered around the clock. For years, I withdrew into agendas and daily plans, and even though my mind remained active, my body continued to break down. By the time I retired at age fifty-five, the imbalance between my mind and body was obvious. I led a toxic lifestyle, not helpful at for my overall health. I began to read books and articles that described health as the connection between mind and body. They all sounded correct, and I needed to explore this and devote time to physical activity.

I joined a gym shortly after I moved to the Central California Coast, and made working-out a priority. It felt good to move my body in new ways and discover muscles I had forgotten. Besides the health benefits I was comforted by seeing others with physical disabilities and realized that being a perfect specimen is not a pre-requisite to working-out. Gradually, I shed my fear of being the only person combating an illness and started to build both strength and pride. My inner smile returned once again.

The fitness center offered Pilates classes. I joined since they are low impact and do not require jumping up and down. Unfortunately, my self-critical, judgmental, and self-defeating "I can't" voice came back. Frustration and discouragement showed its ugly head. I thought I could keep up with the others, but my body refused to do what most members of the class did. Fortunately, the instructor emphasized the importance of non-comparison. "Everybody works at their own pace. The growth is in the effort. Change is individual," she told us. I was relieved to discover there were no expectations. I relaxed. As the weeks continued, I noticed how good it finally felt to use and accept my body and to realize *I can do this.* As I regularly began to use my body, I felt re-united with an old friend. I learned the importance of coordinating my breath with movement and how to focus on core strength. Each exercise helped re-gain stability. The greatest reward was that I accomplished something constructive; my unwarranted feelings of low self-worth began to fade.

It had been close to twenty-five years since my diagnosis of cerebellar ataxia. Western medicine limited me in many ways. Every doctor said the same thing, "there is **no cure.**" That is why I decided to explore alternate healing modalities. In 2010, the fitness center offered restorative yoga, which required the prolonged holding of poses. I was drawn to its slower pace and calming effect. It worked to both soothe my nervous system and cultivate body awareness.

For me, regular exercise is healing in many ways. My stationary bicycle is part of my schedule. It's important to keep my body moving. I believe there needs to be a balance between mind and body. *Healing* may be defined as the curing of an illness or disease. I define *healing* as the relief of distress, the conquering of needless thoughts that cause constant emotional suffering. Until medical research develops a physical cure for cerebellar ataxia, simple, inexpensive and accessible techniques contribute to my health. Exercise is a valuable tool. It is a gift to treasure.

Water Therapy

As my ability to move declined, life became extremely sedentary and difficult. Planning outside events was not worth the effort. Chronic fatigue caused lack of motivation to leave my house. My blank calendar reminded me of the emptiness felt inside. It had once been jam-packed with scheduled meetings and to-do lists. My time at the fitness club had dwindled, and dependence on the cane interfered with any activity. Nothing interested me.

One day a friend suggested a water aquatics class. Thankfully, my former hesitant-self was no longer in control of my decisions. Instead, I went. The water class enabled me to do movements thought to be impossible. For years the fear of falling dominated every move until I learned the benefits of water activity. The water allowed me a new-found freedom of movement. The feelings of *I can* jump up and down, *I can* do jumping jacks, *I can even stand on one leg* thrilled me and I was hooked. A brand new world emerged, and my empty calendar began to fill with scheduled classes.

I came to understand how water exercise coordinates with the workings of the cerebellum. The main function of the cerebellum is to manage motor activities, including balance and coordination. It integrates messages sent from impulse neurons along neural pathways, sending feedback to the body's position in space. Water exercises stress both balance and coordination. The gravity in this liquid environment differs from that on land, supporting a large percentage of body weight. My body's buoyancy in water decreased my fear of falling. If I do lose balance, my hair gets wet; I can live with that. For me, this safety factor allows me to focus on smooth-flowing moves.

When the risk and fear of injury lessened, I concentrated on my exercises, practiced turning, walking sideways and backwards. The aquatics instructor explained that walking in water and reversing directions requires body effort due to resistance. This contributes to brain activity by helping stimulate the neural pathways which send messages to the cerebellum. Anytime a new or different action takes place, new neural pathways can occur. I believe my aquatic exercises build neural pathways and promote fluid movement. My choice is in favor of building-up over breaking-down. The increase in vitality is my reward.

A weekly routine of several different types of exercise, promoted positive effects on my body and mind. I felt subtle differences in mood and a slight increase in my mobility. With added physical exercise, my stronger muscles allow me to walk greater distances and stand for longer periods of time. This has contributed to an increase in social activities, which adds to better, more positive moods. I feel uplifted with greater self-confidence. Now my hours away from home are extended. Finally.

Aside from personal benefits, the water aquatics class allows me to be an example to others. One day upon leaving the pool, a stranger approached me and asked, "Did you have a stroke or something else?" In past years this comment would have offended me. Instead, I answered with confidence, "something else." He quickly replied that he had watched me both in and out of the water and was anxious to share with his friend the difference he witnessed. His friend had recently suffered a stroke and he wanted to encourage him to try water aquatics.

This positive affirmation is also my reward since we are all inter-connected. Following the conversation, I proudly reached for my walker, walked away with joy and my never-ending silent thanks.

The Third Connection: Qigong

*Breathe deeply and slowly, knowing that as the body must be
stretched to do exercise, the heart and mind must be stretched to
stay open to the spirit of life.*
                    Mark Nepo from *The Book of Awakening*

My friend invited me to join her weekly
qigong exercise class. Initially, I was doubtful
because of my poor balance and lack of
coordination. The teacher assured me that I could
be seated to perform the moves, and it would help
improve my balance and stability. This meant I
needed to confront my vanity issues. *Would I look
awkward? Would I appear too different? Would I be
judged?* Although those obstacles were real, I also
knew that qigong incorporates meditative
movements. As Andrew Weil, M.D. writes in the
anthology entitled *The Heart of Healing*: "The root
meaning of *health* is "wholeness," and health
necessarily involves our bodies, minds, and spirits."
Since inner development is as essential to my *health*
as physical, I joined the class. The benefits
outweighed my fears.

Qigong is a form of exercise that mirrors the effortless yet powerful movements in nature. The language speaks of the heaven and earth. They are referred to as flows. One of my favorites is entitled "Cloudy Hands" because of the gentle left and right motions. Each flow releases blocked energy, helps clear stress, and returns vitality to the body. Blood flow improves. Slow, deep breathing sends oxygen to the muscles, and strong muscles equal strong movement. All of the flows require coordination between breath and movement. As I concentrate on my breath I send vital energy up my spinal column. This helps to circulate the qi, or life-energy, and to wake-up my often sluggish and fatigued nervous system. Fatigue is a by-product of my ataxic condition.

I want to do whatever I can to help my balance which is key for my spatial awareness. Simple turns or pivots continue to be challenges, and the simultaneous use of both hands has increased. While qigong flows improve balance and stability, they also help to strengthen my fine motor skills. The emphasis on movement of both sides of the body sends needed messages to the left and right areas of the brain which aids in my use of both hands.

Even though the body and mind are important aspects of healing, the spiritual is also. The integration of body-mind-spirit is a needed practice, and qigong connects all three. With the use of my body, I experience wisdom greater than my small, separate, and changing self, highlighted in the meditative moves. They help lead to the final silent meditation at the end of this class. This brings me inner peace as qigong movements spark a subtle feeling of energy and a connection with my strength and power. It gives me a quiet direction, much like a gentle, flowing stream of water clearing away debris as it travels out to sea. I can flow with it, and find it a valuable tool for staying in touch with my higher self.

I wrote these words in a personal journey dated February 14th, 2016:

> *Not all lessons are learned through pain. My qigong class is infused with joy and acceptance. I connect with a universal rhythm as I move slowly, drift gently. My hands dance through water as I receive this strength.*

This is the energy my body needs in my ongoing search for level ground.

Finding Level Ground

9
Clearing Emotional Debris

Journaling

I found an entry from one of my personal journals written in 2014:

> *It feels as if I'm pushing the same cart uphill. The path looks similar but everything appears steeper and more difficult. The load keeps getting heavier. I feel a strong wind and hear heavy rain.*

These words and feelings had been buried within my subconscious until I discovered the tool of journaling. My ataxia haunted me for years. Despite all medical advances no cure exists, and it is medically categorized as physically degenerative. It is a condition with many challenges to me and my loved ones. While trying to accept my limitation, I knew I did not have to be emotionally paralyzed. I explored alternative methods to cope. My journals helped.

The written word seemed natural. I was always fond of literature and took many English classes in high school and college; I wrote poetry in my 20's and often thought of becoming an author. However, circumstances led me in a different direction. After retiring at age 55 from a 20-year teaching career, I resumed my interest in reading and writing without deadlines, bells, or external pressures to interrupt me. I refused to spend mindless hours watching television or playing games on my computer. A writing class gave me structure and motivation. I was challenged, inspired, and creative. During one of my writing classes, journaling was discussed. That sounded like an endeavor worth pursuing.

Within a short time journaling became a daily routine that was personal and sacred. Self-discipline took hold, and every morning I wrote several pages. With my trusty pen, feelings manifested onto paper. I unpacked suitcases full of shame and guilt that were carried for far too long. No one evaluated or analyzed the quality of my work. My journals did not include a judge or jury, only a happy, joyful, crying me—waiting with open arms. Day after day, I released my feelings, and slowly shed my fears.

My self-image as a victim, co-dependent, and needy, became clear. I also came to understand what kept me depressed, angry, and unwilling to accept my ataxia.

Denial had kept me in a negative, non-nurturing space, so I started to keep a gratitude journal. It was dedicated to everything I felt thankful for in life. My gratitude journal helped me shape positive self-talk, separating facts from self-pity, and replacing any self-absorbed ideas with love and appreciation. My habit of listing what I have in life feels better than dwelling on dark, hopeless thoughts. Positive versus negative. Additionally, I attract people who display that same accepting energy.

The management of self-pity is an ongoing discipline. Self-study persists. Journaling shows me frequent patterns in my behavior such as using discernment versus reacting impulsively with my words, adopting sensitivity rather than being self-absorbed, and practicing patience and trust versus being a skeptic. Focusing on what is, rather than having unrealistic expectations, is my goal. In the words of Ralph Waldo Emerson, "What lies behind us and what lies before us are tiny matters, compared to what lies within us." The activity of journaling is a door into the regions of my thoughts and emotions. It is a personal temple for reflection and a road that leads to self-care.

Sea of Mindfulness: Meditation

`

There has been much tragedy in my life; at least half of it actually happened.

Mark Twain

I travelled down many long, winding roads towards the acceptance of my ataxia. Every stumble and fall triggered anger, unbearable disappointment, and confusion. I filled endless journal pages, with fearful rants on my body's breakdown. *What if this condition never goes away or gets worse? Was this possible? What if...*I didn't understand why simple movements were no longer automatic. This went on year after year like a "broken record." The tape played over and over....Ten years ago I browsed my bookcase and re-read journals written from the time of my early diagnosis. Most of my entries were filled with projections and fears of what could happen in my future. Now in "the future," it sounded like nonsense. As the seasons changed and my bruises continued to increase, I grew tired of those thoughts. I needed to learn new coping skills.

I read various articles about the workings of the brain and recognized a distinction between brain and mind. I used to believe that they shared the same meaning. With time I found the medical definition of brain function differs from mind function. Though there are pictures of the brain, I could not find a diagram of the mind. No scientific facts or graphs pinpoint its location. I realized my ataxia may be impairment of my brain and not of my mind. I could learn to control my mind and influence events in my daily life. Despite degeneration of my brain and the worsening of motor abilities, I had a degree of power over my mind. That was a comforting discovery.

I developed a need to see beyond changing circumstances. I wrote in my gratitude journal daily and began to feel genuine thanks for events in my life. I felt this in an inner place beyond science, beyond words. I longed to express my thanks in all situations. I also read several books that discussed mindfulness, meaning moment by moment, non-judgmental awareness. My identity as a victim had been much too negative. I wanted to reverse my self-critical mannerisms.

Years earlier, I started a discipline called meditation. It was a way to combine mindful awareness with my desire to be grounded in kindness. I needed to be aware of my speech as well as my actions, to live in a friendly universe and not in constant struggle. My daily meditation practice included times of deep silence. Welcome contemplation. Meditation helped clear my mind of needless clutter and I included a greater, loving, universal energy in all of my thoughts. My decisions became more thoughtful of others rather than my usual harsh, demeaning, and me-first, self-absorbed behaviors. I started to mobilize inner resources and celebrate my strengths. I had been stuck for years on the sides of a riverbank, and the currents finally dislodged my fears and carried me into a vast sea—the sea of mindfulness.

Today I can finally admit I have physical challenges because I have learned to befriend both my mind and body. For years needing to be accepted by others blinded me to the truth that my limitations are only one part of me. I am grateful for this awareness and continue to use mindfulness as an essential tool.

Wild Geese

by Mary Oliver

You do not have to be good.
You do not have to walk on your knees
For a hundred miles through the desert, repenting.
You only have to let the soft animal of your body
love what it loves.

Tell me about your despair, yours, and I will tell you mine.
Meanwhile the world goes on.
Meanwhile the sun and the clear pebbles of the rain
are moving across the landscapes,
over the prairies and the deep trees,
the mountains and the rivers.

Meanwhile the wild geese, high in the clean blue air,
are heading home again.
Whoever you are, no matter how lonely,
the world offers itself to your imagination,
calls to you like the wild geese, harsh and exciting —
over and over announcing your place
in the family of things.

10
Level Ground

My Acceptance of Loss

Faith is taking the first step even when you don't see the whole staircase.

Martin Luther King, Jr.

The loss of mobility is emotionally painful. My ataxia is filled with never ending obstacles. I am reminded with each stumble or fall. Just two simple steps have become a challenge. Slower movements and grabbing for added support have helped, however most of my original fears remain. The difference between then and now is I've learned to accept and manage my condition.

I refer again to Elisabeth Kubler-Ross' studies on loss. A loss includes five stages: **denial, anger, bargaining, depression,** and finally, **acceptance**. They do not occur sequentially and can recur when least expected. A physical disability is definitely a loss. I experienced denial, anger, and depression during the onset of my body's breakdown, and again as each motor skill faded. At first I retreated from social functions, snapped at long-time friends who volunteered advice or assistance, and refused to even look at the dreaded blue wheelchair symbol.

When I read that bargaining was an attempt to plead for a reversal of events and a common response in loss—I froze and wondered--*who is listening to my private moments? God, please hear me… Please, make it change, please, I promise. If only….* Ever since my ataxia symptoms surfaced, I would attempt to follow all the socially-accepted rules. I vowed to be kind, helpful, and never again use harmful words. I hoped everything would change and be magically reversed. I thought that bargaining was my way out. I never understood or considered acceptance. I only had an idea of the word. I never felt it in my heart. I needed to travel through many inner doors before I understood acceptance.

One door was shifting my beliefs from a divine judgmental, punishing God into a loving, kind, and accepting universal energy. Another door has been the acceptance of my body—as is. I now realize that who I am is greater than diagrams, charts, or medical tests. When I first lost my abilities, I turned to science for answers, always hoping it might get fixed and go away. But as time went on and doctors repeatedly told me "sorry, learn to live with it," I felt as if my life ended. I was screaming from within, *"I'm melting, I'm melting."* It was twenty years and eight chapters later before acceptance took root.

A third door towards acceptance requires faith and trust. My faith helped me understand that who I am is greater than I had thought. I used to believe my condition was self-imposed and somehow my fault. The fact is a disability is not a punishment. I did nothing wrong. It is what it is. Acceptance requires that I look beyond my denial, anger, and depression to honestly examine my strengths and weaknesses. It requires my continual willingness to embrace what is known and not known, and demands that I widen my focus from momentary discomforts to a broader realistic worldview. From "poor little me" to healing strength.

Acceptance generated my faith in possibilities. It is why I must and will actively help raise awareness for people with this condition.

Acceptance is why I keep joy in my heart and a smile on my face. Acceptance is the ability to recognize, communicate, and open myself to both the joys and pains of this world. It is my willingness to allow the mysteries in life to flow through me. It is why I'll always believe there are greater reasons beyond what I've learned. All experiences in life have meanings which often differ from our expectations. Ultimately, my physical loss has prompted me to understand realities I might have never known, and a faithful commitment to taking that next step.

May the ground always be level.

Acceptance Leads to Courage

It takes courage, to step out of the fray, it takes courage to do anything that's necessary…

Pico Iyer from *Art of Stillness*

Ataxia has been part of my life for more than thirty years. I have lived with numerous challenges: cuts and bruises, broken bones, injured ribs, and torn ligaments and muscles. Along the way, I have hiked many hills and valleys. Each time, I felt shame and disappointment. I have hoped, prayed, and wished for my ataxia to go away. Many doctors told me, "Sorry, no cure. Learn to live with it." Some loved ones and friends understood my struggles; others did not. Yet despite everything, I refused to define myself as wounded, learned to reach beyond limitations, and to find the fruit on the tree. As my grandmother taught me, "enough already."

That was in the past. For years I've been on a slow inner journey towards acceptance of my authenticity. What I defined as truth has evolved. The mysteries in nature, my body, and other people have guided me. When I received my ataxia diagnosis, I felt my life had ended. But as the years unfolded, my thoughts and choices have changed. Being happy is a choice. I have learned to discern situations and decide what works in my favor, carefully decide what is best for my body, and choose my daily activities, environment, and the people who surround me. Positive energy is crucial.

When I chose to live on my own, I sacrificed luxuries and around-the-clock help that I thought was needed. I was frightened. I would have to live on a tight budget, arrange for transportation, cook, clean, and practice never-ending self-care. My fears were endless. *What if I fall? What if I'm too weak to cook? How will I get my groceries?* I was terrified. I researched available ADA sites, and became empowered to shop for a new walker. It was a non-stop job; however, I discovered that the benefits cancelled all of my worries. Once I started to take courageous and positive steps, my friends and family showered me with love and support. My social life expanded. My calendar filled with activities. My energy increased, and I attained inner peace and self-worth that I had denied myself for too long. This is my story of stepping out. It can be yours if you choose a life based on faith and trust rather than on fear.

I spent many years trying to live up to other people's definition of courage. Instead, I learned that everyone must find their own courage-course. No other person can claim to know what you want or need. Other people can nurture and encourage, but only you can decide what is best. It took many years of struggles, drama, and poor choices before I reached that awareness.

It takes courage to move beyond the familiar, yet we all have the ability to be comfortable with ourselves. My heartfelt prayers, thoughts, and wishes go to my fellow ataxians, or to anyone dealing with challenges. Courage is an obtainable gift. May we all choose to accept and receive this gift. May we all find level ground.

There is no ending to my story but rather the unfolding of physical loss and the gradual acceptance of a reality that grows in the human heart. This story is both the rot and the perfume of life; the sweet and sour, the surface and deep, mine and maybe yours.

Final Thoughts

Initially the stories in this book were written for myself only and not for publication. I felt ashamed, confused, disappointed, and saddened to admit a disability had overtaken my life. The thought that my ataxia had no cure paralyzed my thinking and limited me to victimhood for many years. Trapped by my doubts and a multitude of fears, I refused and was unable to see anything but darkness. As I started to read and listen to other people's stories, my feelings became less about myself as an isolated victim and more about compassion. I had no idea that so many people shared similar trials and am humbled whenever I read or hear their everyday battles and their successes. They fill me with hope and the desire to find my own level ground.

I write this book to tell my life story to fellow ataxians or to anyone facing physical challenge. I wanted to emphasize how common feelings and experiences exist among those who suffer mobility loss and suggest effective coping skills. When I learned about the stages of loss, my experiences began to make sense and my writing took on new meaning. I replaced "telling about" with "sharing with." Writing this book helped me to shed my shame and denial, and to voice my previous fears in a public way, layer by layer, chapter by chapter. As each one of my stories and poems appeared on paper, my authentic-self grew stronger and stronger. I found some "level ground," and for that alone, I extend my heartfelt thanks.

Finding Level Ground refers to a human journey through levels of grief. Hopefully, we reach the final stage of acceptance. Everyone has the ability to transform from victim to victorious. The Beatles once sang the song, "It Don't Come Easy." It took me years to find my starting line. I recommend we begin on this path towards acceptance now rather than later. My goal is to always embrace reality, and move forward. This book is my affirmation.

Gratitudes

I extend my heartfelt thanks to everyone who gave me the encouragement to print these words. I believe we are all stars in the same constellation; lights in the same sky. Helen Keller once wrote, "Alone we can do so little; together we can do so much." This book is a testament that when we all work together, the possibilities are endless. I send my thanks to all who taught me how to share, and to the many wise teachers, writers, and poets for their inspirational ideas and words.

I thank my writing friends Ila June Brunner and Anne Brazil for our in-depth weekly group meetings, and I am deeply grateful for all the input provided by my other group writers. Thanks to Lenny Erickson for her invaluable editing skills. I extend thanks to my teacher, Diane Halsted, for guiding me on my path of writing. I give special thanks to both my loving sons for always being there for me. My family and friends are my guiding lights.

I thank those people in the scientific community who dedicate time and expertise to search for cures for all ataxias and related diseases.

I thank those that help to spread awareness. Finally, I thank the reader for purchasing this book. Proceeds will be donated to enable further research so that no-one will ever have to hear, "Sorry, no cure."

I send out love and healing prayers to those who suffer. May we all continue to help one another as we search for level ground.

Finding Level Ground

cover photo
  by Tom Levi

formatting
  by Anne Brazil

TIMELESS LOVE

Not years nor words
can change the connection
of our hearts
Nothing between me and the white
fire of the stars separates
your hands from mine —
we cling to our stories
become tangled in our daily webs,
lost in details of time.
For brief moments we brush against
each other, smile,
then turn away

taking bits to remember
and weave into memory.

Sharing the Shawl

I travelled down many chilly roads
searching for answers, asking praying,
begging, hoping—looked under many

rocks. Scientific stacks of findings,
medical notepads cluttered my paths. '
I finally found my shielded shawl—

inner strength, a heart encased in faith
and trust—now passed along to cover
your doubts and fears. May you wear it to

find your acceptance. May you feel the threads
of this human tapestry warming
your heart. May you find comfort as you

climb the hills. May you have the courage
to travel through the valleys where the
victim lies in wait—remembering

that wherever you walk, courage and
light will forever guide your footsteps.
I pass to you my shawl of acceptance.

Bibliography and Resources for Further Study

Texts

Barbara Bates, M.D.
"A Guide to Physical Examination and History
Taking" – 4th Edition
J.B. Lippencott Co., Philadelphia, 1983

Frederic and Mary Ann Brussat
"Spiritual Literacy"-an anthology-
A Touchstone Book - Published by Simon &
Schuster, 1998

Edited by Dawson Church
"The Heart of Healing" -an anthology-
Elite Books, 2004

Ram Dass
"Still Here: Embracing Aging, Changing, Dying"
Penguin Group – Riverhead Books, 2000

Norman Doidge, M.D.
"The Brain That Changes Itself"
Penguin Books, 2007

Norman Doidge, M.D.
"The Brain's Way of Healing"
Penguin Books, 2015

Pico Iyer
"The Art of Stillness"
TED Books – Simon & Schuster, 2014

Elisabeth Kubler-Ross
"On Grief & Grieving: Finding the Meaning of
Grief Through the Five Stages of Loss"
SCRIBNER – A Division of Simon & Shuster, Inc.,
2014

Darcy Leech
"From My Mother: Surviving and Thriving in a
Family Ravaged by
                    Genetic Disease
eLectio Books, Little Elm, Texas, 2016

Kristin Neff, Ph.D
"Self-Compassion"
William Morrow Publisher, 2015

Mark Nepo
"The Book of Awakening"
Conari Press, 2000

Jon Kabat-Zinn
"Full Catastrophe Living: Using the
Wisdom of Your Body and Mind to
Face Stress, Pain, and Illness"
Bantam Books, 2013

Jon Kabat-Zinn
"Wherever You Go, There You Are"
Hyperion Books, 1994

Journals

Cerebellum & Ataxias
Journal of Neurology
Neurology Now
Practical Neurology
The Cerebellum

NAF (National Ataxia Foundation): *Generations*
Reader-friendly

Online Resources

www.waterpts.com/news/2015/8/12/8
  "Benefits of Aquatic Therapy-How Water Works"
www.athleticpt.com/blog/physicaltherapy
  "6 Aquatic Physical Therapy Exercises to Improve
    Your Balance"
www.energyarts.com
  "What is Qigong?"
www.webmd.com/fitnessexercise
  "Tai chi and Qigong"
www.goodtherapy.org/blog
  "Journaling to the Center: How Writing
Encourages Insight and Healing"

ADA Travel Resources

"Travel Near and Travel Far: Step Out of Your Disability!"
Terry Scott Cohen, Barry M. Cohen, Ph.D.
Wishing Well Publishing, Clearwater, Florida, 2015
TerrysChallenges.com

AbilitiesEXPO.com
   Look to these trailblazers for advice.

www.accomable.com
   online platform enabling people with disabilities to find accessible accommodation all over the world.

www.easyaccess.com
   Cruise planners (easy accessible travel)

www.ricksteves.com/traveltips
   "Tips for Travelers With Disabilities"

www.disabilityrights-cdr.org
   many travel resources listed

Contact National and Federal Parks for ADA accessibility.

GET OUT and ENJOY YOUR WORLD

Made in the USA
Coppell, TX
06 June 2021